The Good Old Days
Traditions of Rural America

How dear to my heart are the scenes of my childhood,
When fond recollection presents them to view!
The orchard the meadow the deep tangled wildwood,
And every loved spot which my infancy knew.

The wide spreading pond and the mill that stood by it,
The bridge and the rock where the cataract fell.
The cot of my father the dairy house nigh it,
And e'en the rude bucket that hung in the well.

The old oaken bucket, The iron bound bucket,
The moss covered bucket that hung in the well.

IDEALS PUBLICATIONS INCORPORATED
NASHVILLE, TENNESSEE

ACKNOWLEDGMENTS

AUTUMN and WINTER by Edgar A. Guest. Used by permission of the author's estate; CHURCH SUPPERS by Evan Jones. Copyright © 1976 by Evan Jones; APPLE BUTTER from *THE GOOD OLD DAYS* by R.J. McGinnis copyright © 1960 by F&W Publishing Corporation; FADING MEMORIES OF THE FAMILY FARM by Jay Scriba reprinted from *The Milwaukee Journal*, June 6, 1971; Our sincere thanks to the following authors whom we were unable to contact: Elsie Natalie Brady for WHEN GRANPA WALKED TO SCHOOL; Inga Gilson Caldwell for OLD BARNS; Rosa Mary Clausen-Mohr for OUTDATED; Marion Doyle for I LIKE BARNS; Maud M. Doolittle for UNSUNG FRAGRANCE; Harriet Feltham for WINTER WASHDAY; Edwin Osgood Grover for THE COUNTRY BOY'S CREED; Nelle Hardgrove for TIME REPEATING; Mary Nell Johnson for HAY BALING WITH HORSES; Roy Z. Kemp for PLANTING; Brian F. King for MAPLE SUGAR TIME; Henry B. Knox for SONG OF THE MEADOWLARK; May Benedict Maye for THE OLDEST THINGS; Mrs. Ollie B. McArthur for MAY DAY; Truda McCoy for KITCHEN MEMORIES; Maysie Tuley Newsom for ALWAYS REMEMBERING; Cynthia L. Pryor for WINTER LONG AGO; T. M. Rutledge for APPLE PIE; Bertha L. Stone for DANDELIONS; Lloyd Stone for HOME FROM SCHOOL; and Rachel Lumpkin Wyly for OTHER SPRINGS.

ISBN 0-8249-4061-X

Published by Ideals Publications Incorporated
565 Marriott Drive
Nashville, TN 37214

The text type was set in Galliard.
The display type was set in Caflisch Script.
Color separations were made by Precision Color Graphics Ltd. of New Berlin, WI

Cover Photo: Autumn in the Blue Ridge Mountains near Cove Creek, Watauga County, North
Carolina. Photography by Norman Poole

Contents

SPRING

By the Light of the Silvery Moon

ED MADDEN

GUS EDWARDS

Arranged by Dick Torrans

1. Place park, scene dark, Sil - v'ry moon is shin - ing thru the trees;
2. Act two scene new, Ros - es bloom - ing all a - round the place;

Cast two, me, you, Sound of kiss - es float - ing on the breeze.—
Cast three, you, me, Preach - er with a sol - emn look - ing face.—

Act one, be - gun, Di - a - logue, "Where would you like to spoon?"
Choir sings, bell rings, Preach - er: "You are wed for - ev - er - more!"

My cue, with you, Un - der - neath the sil - v'ry moon. By the
Act two, all through, Ev - 'ry night the same en - core.

As the Heart Remembers Spring

Betty W. Stoffel

Some will be remembered
For the fortunes of their fame,
And some will be remembered
For the naming of a name,
But you will be remembered
As the heart remembers spring,
As the mind remembers beauty,
And the soul each lovely thing.
You have been skies of April,
And fragrant breath of May,
And like the season's coming,
Warm-spirited and gay.
You have given freely
Of the beauty of your heart,
And you have made of friendship
Not a gesture but an art.
You have been as selfless
In the gracious things you do
As the sun that shares its kisses,
As the night that shares its dew.
You have planted roses
In lives that lay so bare,
You have sown encouragement
To those who knew despair.
By spirit's inner beauty
In every lovely thing,
You will be remembered
As the heart remembers spring!

Papa's House

Hildred Carlsen

I remember as a child going to Papa's house—
Memories, yes, memories of bygone days.
Memories of walking down the dusty gravel road,
Of the mailbox where we turned down the lane,
Of crossing the creek on a foot log,
Of the storm cellar.
Memories of the farm animals in the barnyard,
Of Ole Rube barking to announce our arrival,
Yes, memories of visiting the old farmhouse, Papa's house.

In memories, I often return to Papa's house,
Memories of fresh-turned earth,
Of spring planting,
Of walks with Grandma,
Of gathering poke greens, mushrooms, and dandelions.
Memories of the smell of wild honeysuckle,
Of blackberries in bloom,
Of rooster-head violets—
Yes, memories of the beauty of the springtime at Papa's house.

PHOTO RIGHT:
DANDELIONS AND FARMHOUSE IN SPRING
BERKSHIRE GARDENS
STOCKBRIDGE, MASSACHUSETTS
JOHNSON'S PHOTOGRAPHY

A Country Boy's Creed

Edwin Osgood Grover

I believe that the country which God made is more beautiful than the city which man made; that life out-of-doors and in touch with the earth is the natural life of man. I believe that work is work wherever we find it, but that work with nature is more inspiring than work with the most intricate machinery.

I believe that the dignity of labor depends not on what you do, but on how you do it; that opportunity comes to a boy on the farm as often as to a boy in the city; that life is larger and freer and happier on the farm than in the town; that my success depends not upon my location, but upon myself; not upon my dreams, but upon what I actually do; not upon luck, but upon pluck.

I believe in working when you work and in playing when you play, and in giving and demanding a square deal in every act of life. ❦

Wintergreen Berries in the Springtime

Helen Colwell Oakley

Discovering a tiny clump of bright red wintergreen berries on the slopes of the meadow in the early spring was a magical time when I was a youngster on the farm. Before all traces of snow had vanished from the mountainside we cherished one of the earliest signs of spring: delicious red wintergreen berries popping out of the greening foliage, temptingly inviting us with their beauty and sweet aroma. Children of all ages searched excitedly for the berry treats—sometimes partially hidden by lush green leaves—then savored them one after the other until they could sample no more. The women were more practical: they would sample one or two then gather the berries, with the stems and leaves attached, and carefully put them in baskets to carry home.

Mom baked a springtime cake, garnishing it lavishly with pink frosting and the tiny red berries and shiny green leaves of the wintergreen. Mom also put the wintergreen leaves in bottles with a preservative and stored them in the pantry or the fruit cellar for flavoring cakes, cookies, and desserts later on. Some of the mothers made delicious candies, flavored with this tasty wintergreen and tinted a lovely shade of green. Others preserved the leaves for medicinal purposes: the herb-like leaves were a family remedy for a tummy- or earache and many other common pains. The concoction was rather pleasant to take for a tummy ache—sweet and deliciously fragrant.

As springtime arrives in the country once again, I remember the days of yesteryear when we searched for the delicate white bell-shaped flowers upon our slopes above the meadows. Soon there would be one of the best springtime treats of all—a mountainside covered with spicy red wintergreen berries. ❧

PHOTO LEFT:
SPRING HILLSIDE
KENTUCKY
ADAM JONES

Maple Sugar Time

Brian F. King

When winter flees from rural lanes
To seek retreat in windswept hills,
And brooklets chant the sweet refrains
That speak of waiting daffodils.
Then bright plateaus of melting snow
Guard vales where sugar maples grow.

By old stone walls the maple glades
Stand proudly in the joyous sun:
The rich designs of light and shade
Grace peaceful groves where spigots run
And weathered buckets ring each tree
Where silver sap is flowing free.

No small city boy has ever shared
The bliss that reaches peaks sublime
When country children race, prepared
To harvest sap in sugar time;
Nor does he know the golden glow
Of boiling sap on sugar snow.

Now spring proclaims her majesty
In glens where nectar trickles clear,
Where sugar makers hold the key
To nature's sweetest time of year.
It's spring and perfumed mists arise
From maple groves to smiling skies.

PHOTO OPPOSITE:
A ROW OF SUGAR MAPLES

PHOTO BELOW:
COLLECTING MAPLE SAP
STATE HISTORICAL SOCIETY OF WISCONSIN

Nostalgia

Anne Tilley Franz

Some glad, blue morning I shall come
And stand again beneath the plum
That grows beside the old rock wall
And see the snow-white petals fall.

There'll be a robin in the tree,
And spider ships on a meadow sea;
I'll see the sun in splendor rise
And bathe in gold the morning skies.

I'll dream beside the lily pond;
Relive each precious day that's gone.
Again, I'll breathe the mountain air
And pray to Him this little prayer:

O, let me know this scene again—
A plum tree washed in April rain,
The rustic strength of the ancient wall,
And peace, dear God, when shadows fall.

PHOTO LEFT:
WINDMILL WITH FLOWERING SHRUB AND
STONE WALL
JAMESTOWN, RHODE ISLAND
JOHNSON'S PHOTOGRAPHY

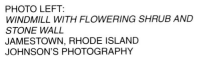

Early spring is the time to prepare the kitchen herb garden, just outside the kitchen door. One of the most versatile herbs is *Rosmarinus officinalis,* or common rosemary. This herb grows about four feet tall and has silvery green, needle-shaped leaves. It grows well in the garden or, if you prefer, plant it in a pot. Prune rosemary often to keep it bushy.

Rosemary symbolized kindness and constancy. Legend has it that rosemary will not grow for anyone who has been unkind or unfaithful. Shakespeare, in *Hamlet*, has the kind Ophelia saying, "There's rosemary; that's for remembrance; pray, love, remember."

Preserve those weeds around your country property or out where a barn once was. Brush and weeds can be useful to butterflies. They feed on milkweed, thistles, daisies, dandelions, clover, and asters. And butterflies lay their eggs in weeds.

Another popular herb is *Majorana hortensis,* or sweet marjoram. This herb grows well in the garden, in window boxes, or in pots. Marjoram can grow twelve to eighteen inches and produces dainty white, pale pink, or lavender flowers.

Sweet marjoram was said to have been planted on Mount Olympus by Venus herself. A choice of the goddess, marjoram is now often used to flavor soups and salads.

Frosted Easter Egg Rolls

Try these delicious rolls for an Easter weekend treat. Thaw a one-pound loaf of frozen cinnamon or raisin bread dough. Let rise until doubled in size. Break off pieces of dough and roll into the shape of an egg. Place "eggs" in a lightly greased pie pan and bake at 350° until lightly browned, about 25 minutes. Cool on a wire rack. When cool, decorate eggs with colored frostings and colored sprinkles.

The word verbena means "sacred bough" and legend says this herb was essential to Druid rituals. It was also used by ancient herbalists as a cure for everything from jaundice to miscarriage.

Verbena hortensis blooms continuously from June to late fall; the plant is about eight inches high and produces white, red, or lilac flowers in broad, flat clusters.

Lavender blue, dilly, dilly,
Lavender green,
When I am king, dilly, dilly,
You shall be queen.

So promises an old nursery rhyme about a most romantic plant, *Lavundula spica*. Lavender grows about two feet high and has gray-green curling leaves and pale violet flowers. Lavender is the fragrant herb of choice for sachets and lingerie drawers.

Pick dandelion greens early in the year; as the season progresses, they will become increasingly bitter. As long as the plant has not blossomed, however, the greens are edible. If the bitterness is objectionable, reduce this somewhat by soaking overnight in cold water with a teaspoon of salt and juice of half a lemon. Next morning, drain and use in the usual way. Or, cover the greens with boiling water; then drain the water before cooking them according to the recipe.

To cook dandelion greens, gather 1 to 1½ gallons tender dandelion greens. Wash well. Set aside. Place a ham hock in a large kettle and cover with water; bring to a boil. Simmer until the broth is rich and the meat tender, about 1 hour. Add the cleaned greens to the kettle; cover and simmer gently until the greens are tender and well flavored, about 1 hour. Season greens with salt and pepper, as needed, during the cooking. Serve greens in a hot tureen with the pot liquor poured over them. Serve with cornbread or cornmeal dumplings and vinegar. Serves 8.

Pick plump, ripe strawberries from early to late May, by following the signs to the farms where the roadsides proudly proclaim: "Pick your own." Doesn't everyone alway pick about four times the number of berries their family can eat while dreaming of strawberry jam, jelly, frozen pies, frozen berries. Once home, however, all thoughts of putting up the fruit to enjoy it all winter give way to daily schedules. Most of us simply give away the over supply to our neighbors and friends. In the great scheme of things, perhaps "putting up" friends makes a more valuable addition to our lives than "putting up" those jars of jelly.

Planting

Roy Z. Kemp

Upon a frosty morn the eager team
Stamp their feet and blow out breath of smoky steam
That curls and rises up, a billowing
Of whispy fog that's like some living thing.

The field is waking once again to life
And waiting for the plow's bright shining knife
To ridge its furrows, lay its straightened rows
For seed and suckling, for every thing that grows.

The farmer grasps the handles of his plow,
The reins across one shoulder; he knows how
To make his team plunge quickly to its work
Without a whimper, stall, or any shirk.

The hardened earth gives way before the blade—
The world needs food; here good food is made.

PHOTO LEFT:
LONE ELM TREE AND CORNFIELD IN SPRING
EAST CRAFTSBURY, VERMONT
JOHNSON'S PHOTOGRAPHY

A Springtime Adventure

Charles L. Martin

There is something about the springtime that carries me back to the days when my father and I would walk in the country along dirt roads that seemed to melt into the hills and countryside. Everything was alive with the goodness and the beauty of the season. To my child's mind, these walks were a great game and full of adventure. It was a time when imagination flared and nothing could possibly go wrong.

During our walks we would stop along the road to admire the beauty of the wild flowering trees—the crab apple, plum, red haw, and mulberry that would later provide us with delicious fruits when spring gave way to summer and then fall. The fragrance of the blossoms, coupled with my own excitement, filled the air with springtime wonder. The wild ground flowers—violets, sweet williams, mayapples, Dutchman's-breeches, and columbine—blooming in abundance, displayed color to rival the illustrations of a storybook.

The small creeks and streams were filled with green watercress; the mating calls of the frogs floated on the air. We walked along old deserted roads, often passing the remains of an old house, with only the brick chimney and the foundation to bear witness to the home that had once been.

I remember an old bridge that fascinated me with its faded, weather-beaten sign warning us to cross "at our own risk." The wooden pilings that once supported the bridge still stood tall, but the floorboards had disappeared, the victims of time and the weather.

My father would point out places of interest such as groves of huge elm, hackberry, mighty oak, and walnut trees that soared toward the sky. He explained how in autumn the ground would be covered by their acorns and walnuts, providing food for the animals, and a new generation of trees. After each adventure we would head towards home, but not before cutting a few branches of wild crab apple blossoms or a small bouquet of violets or sweet william for my mother. She would arrange them in a vase and place the colorful display on the dining room table for all to admire.

It seems that there was more closeness in families back then—more time for quiet country walks. In those days, the simple things had more meaning and families lived together without fear, guided by faith in one another and in God. There was a security and a peace of mind that we all felt. Today, much of that is just a cherished memory—like my springtime walks with Father. ❧

Old Barns

Glenn Ward Dresbach

The swallows, divers in blue pools of air,
Drift back to old eaves mellow with the sun,
And on its knoll the old barn seems to stare
No more with empty windows. Through it run
Winds, stirring fragrance in the shadowed mows
That once had overflowed with meadow hay,
And pigeons, strutting through their changeless vows,
Possess the sagging roof that suns today.

If some old man could watch it for awhile
Across the lane or by the pasture brook,
I think he would remember with a smile
And venture closer for a wistful look
How structures still may sag but timbers hold
Their mellow strength—and friends they had of old.

PHOTO RIGHT:
RED FLOWERING DOGWOOD AND BARN DOORWAY
GREENFIELD HILL, CONNECTICUT
JOHNSON'S PHOTOGRAPHY

Dear Mona

Maud Williams Burgess

This has been a nice Easter Sunday, a little on the cool side, but until late this afternoon it was bright and sunny. Thank you for the lovely Easter card.

I will try to give you a few of my most cherished memories from when I was a little girl your age. I lived on a farm until I was nine years old, the oldest of Mother and Father's six children—four girls and two boys. I was Mother's little helper where the children were concerned. My task was to keep the oldest ones outside during nice weather. My favorite place for them was across the road from the house in a nice pinewooded place. I would give each of them a hoe, rake, ax—yes, I always carried the ax—anything with a long handle we could throw over our shoulders and play soldier. I enjoyed that quite a bit and so did the children. I often had as many as eight or ten in line behind me, because often Mother would have a neighbor woman bring her children to spend the afternoon. While the mothers quilted, patched, knitted, or crocheted, we children hustled across the road to play.

I enjoyed helping my father feed the stock at night, especially the little pigs. I wasn't allowed near the cows or horses for fear of being kicked, but followed my father with a little basket on my arm filled with ears of dried corn. As long as I was allowed to help him with anything, I felt like a big girl. I'm sure you've helped gather eggs. I enjoyed that, too, but my favorite pastime was following along behind a man plowing, kicking that fresh-plowed earth with my bare feet. Even at my ripe old age I think I would thoroughly enjoy that now. There is something about the feel of fresh earth that is so invigorating.

My first school days were exciting. My sister and I rode a horse bareback three miles to a one-room schoolhouse, dinner bucket on one side of the horse's head and horse food on the other side. When we reached the schoolhouse, the teacher took us off and took care of our horse. She sent us on our way about four o'clock in the afternoon. Sometimes it was dark when we got home, for our old horse would graze on the side of the road. I guess he didn't always get enough dinner!

Another good time was in the spring of the year when they had log-rolling—although I never saw any logs rolled! In the spring, a farmer would decide he wanted to take in more land to cultivate, but there would be many, many stumps to be removed. All his neighbors far and near would travel to help him. The men would usually go a day ahead of time and "blow stump"—with what, I never heard, because that was a long, long time ago. When the log-rolling day came, the men left home early, leaving mothers and children to pack in covered wagons all kinds of food they had been preparing for days, gather up the children that had been scrubbed until they shone, put them in the old wagon, and drive to the neighbor's farm. Funny thing, I can still hear those men in that field singing lustily as we neared the farm, the mules and oxen pulling, pulling, pulling stumps and piling them to be burned later. And that, Mona, was log-rolling in Arkansas! . . .

I was just a little girl on the farm at your age with no radio, TV, moving pictures, street-cars, buses, or automobiles like you have today. But we were a happy bunch of little girls living and doing for each other with what we had; it took so little to make us happy. I look back on those days of long ago and just think we were so very happy. . . .

Good luck and lots of love,

Nanny

Recipe for Memories

Rev. Elizabeth J. Walton

Memories are made from these:
Bubbling brooks and old pine trees,
Violets in the early spring,
The sweet, clear song that the bluebirds sing.
Memories are mixtures rare
Of familiar odors in the air—
Like the smell of wood fires burning bright
And home-baked beans on a Saturday night.
The sniff of rain on an April day
And the hint of pine and new mown hay.
To make a batch of memory sweet
You must have love and joy complete.
You must have home and loved ones dear:
A drop of laughter, a smile, a tear.
Mixed together they're sure to please—
For memories are made of these.

PHOTO OPPOSITE:
DAIRY FARM
NEAR LEXINGTON, KENTUCKY
ADAM JONES

May Day

Mrs. Ollie D. McArthur

The old school yard across the street
Is filled today with children's feet;
The pole is raised, the ribbons fly,
And garlands of flowers hang nearby.
In dainty frocks, some with curls,
Are many lovely little girls,
And the little boys in suits of white
Complete the scene—a wondrous sight!
There a mother stands—so proud
Of her little one, there in the crowd.
"Welcome, sweet Springtime" fills the air—
Now hushed the song; the Queen is there!

I gaze and gaze at the scene today
But my thoughts go back to another May
When a little boy stood in the very same place
And shyly glanced at the May Queen's face;
For the fair one who was crowned that day
Had stolen his child's heart away,
And he was glad for the others to see
What a beautiful Queen his girl could be.
When she chanced to throw a smile his way
He flushed a bit and glanced away;
Even now he sees—though he's long since grown,
How lovely she looked on her May Day throne.

PHOTO ABOVE:
*LILACS AND TOWN CLERK'S
OFFICE IN SPRING*
HEBRON, NEW HAMPSHIRE
JOHNSON'S PHOTOGRAPHY

May Baskets and Memories

Margaret E. Shiner

The rain came down in a gentle mist
And the lilac tree bloomed near.
It made me sigh as I lived again
Those days of another year.

For lilac time was May Day time
With excitement for everyone—
Not quite like Christmas or the Fourth of July—
But, oh, it was such fun!

We'd work for days in order to make
The prettiest basket we could;
Then we'd fill it full of lilacs sweet
And things we thought were good:

Candy, gum, and some tiny surprise
Tucked under the lilac cover.
Then we'd hide our names deep inside
Playing the secret lover.

We'd place the basket beside the door
And knock as loud as we dared
Then run as fast as our legs would go
Pretending we were scared.

Yet secretly hoping all the while
That we would be caught, not missed,
For if you were caught by the one you liked
That was the one you kissed!

Rain and lilacs and May time now
Give memory a sudden start,
For the man I married so long ago
Was my dear May Day sweetheart.

The House by the Side of the Road

Sam Walter Foss

There are hermit souls that live withdrawn
In the place of their self-content;
There are souls, like stars, that dwell apart,
In a fellowless firmament;
There are pioneer souls that blaze their paths
Where highways never ran—
But let me live by the side of the road
And be a friend to man.

Let me live in a house by the side of the road,
Where the race of men go by—
The men who are good and the men who are bad,
As good and as bad as I.
I would not sit in the scorner's seat,
Or hurl the cynic's ban—
Let me live in a house by the side of the road
And be a friend to man.

I see from my house by the side of the road,
By the side of the highway of life,
The men who press with the ardor of hope,
The men who are faint with the strife.
But I turn not away from their smiles nor their tears,
Both parts of an infinite plan—
Let me live in a house by the side of the road
And be a friend to man.

I know there are brook-gladdened meadows ahead,
And mountains of wearisome height;
That the road passes on through the long afternoon
And stretches away to the night.
But still I rejoice when the travelers rejoice,
And weep with the strangers that moan,
Nor live in my house by the side of the road
Like a man who dwells alone.

PHOTO ABOVE:
IRISES AND BACK SHED
STONE'S THROW GARDENS
EAST CRAFTSBURY, VERMONT
JOHNSON'S PHOTOGRAPHY

Let me live in my house by the side of the road,
It's here the race of men go by—
They are good, they are bad, they are weak, they are strong,
Wise, foolish—so am I;
Then why should I sit in the scorner's seat,
Or hurl the cynic's ban?
Let me live in my house by the side of the road
And be a friend to man.

SUMMER

In the Good Old Summer Time

REN SHIELDS

GEORGE EVANS
Arranged by Dick Torrans

1. There's a time in each year that we al - ways hold dear, Good old
2. To swim in the pool, you'd play "hook - y" from school, Good old

sum - mer time; With the birds and the trees - es and sweet scent - ed
sum - mer time; You'd play "ring - a - ros - ie" with Jim, Kate and

breez - es, Good old sum - mer time, When your day's work is ov - er then
Jos - ie, Good old sum - mer time, Those days full of pleas - ure we

you are in clov - er, and life is one beau - ti - ful rhyme, No trou - ble an - go
now find - ly treas - ure, when we nev - er thought it a crime, To go steal - ing

Fading Memories of the Family Farm

Jay Scriba

For a restless boy, nothing could match the thrill of a couple of July weeks on the old farm. You awoke to crowing roosters, opening an eye to sun streaming through the cracks in the green shades. Even the bedding was different . . . a patchwork quilt over a rustling corn-shuck mattress and embroidery on the feather pillow (smelling richly of the hen house).

The aunts and uncles, of course, had been up since dawn, milking cows, watering chickens, digging into the crock for pre-fried pork sausage patties, pungent with pepper and sage. There was the smell of Swedish pot coffee and the sound of soft farm talk from the kitchen. Sometimes the milk on our oatmeal was still warm and foaming from the cow.

What to do first? Uncle Charley was hoeing among the sweet corn and cucumbers, stopping now and then to file a bright edge. Later he would be puttering in the garage, where a Kentucky rifle still hung on the wall over a collection of license plates dating back to 1914.

Aunt Grace was pumping one of the old Galenas, filling the smokehouse trough with cold water to cool the milk, butter, and cottage cheese.

Aunt Mary had put on a sunbonnet and stretched stockings over her arms to protect them from the brambles on a blackberrying expedition to Burton's woods. . . .

For a start, we generally went off on our own, out to the barnyard to pump the pig and horse troughs full, eager to pat a snuffling mare on her velvet nose. The little pigs were warier, standing stiff legged and alert, set for playful, squealing flight at the wave of a new straw hat.

We might go into the corncrib in the new red barn to shell a few ears in the rackety hand sheller. Or we might climb into the heaped wheat in the grain bin . . . the most comfortable lounging cushion in the world . . . and chew a handful of kernels until they became a chaffy gum. . . .

Through the rest of the morning we might ride on one of the big horses while Uncle Charley plowed corn, clinging desperately to the fly netting as Big Jack shook his hide to dislodge a horsefly. The thing to do was grip hard on the brass collar balls and never look down.

Then it would be noon with Aunt Grace ringing the cowbell. Time to go to the rain barrel, swat the wash pan hard to drive down the swarming mosquito wigglers and wash up, maybe stick your cowlick under the icy pump water. (The wooden pump deck stood among the moss, wild mint, and the purple flowers on the ground.)

Dinner was substantial, with dark slices of ham down from the attic, bowls of mashed potatoes with cream gravy, watermelon pickles, spiced peaches, iced tea, a firm flaky slice of cherry or apple pie. (Always, by 11 a.m., there was a pie cooling in the kitchen window.)

After the pie, there was time for a nap on the creaking porch swing next to the sweet honeysuckle, or in the hammock next to the truck patch, which produced gooseberries, currants, chives, asparagus—a gourmet's dream of fresh vegetables.

The ninety-degree afternoon heat might find us with an oilcan, filling the cups on a dilapidated corn planter, mower, and other machinery in the implement shed. We would hunt eggs by the hour in the tangled goldenrod and jimsonweed, sometimes returning in triumph with whole clutches.

By four o'clock it was time for coffee and a slice of pink-iced angel cake. Aunt Mary would be back with a milk pail full of glistening blackberries and Uncle Charley would tell Aunt

PHOTO ABOVE:
YELLOW BARN AND CORNFIELD IN SUMMER
SHARON, VERMONT
JOHNSON'S PHOTOGRAPHY

Grace that the wind had shifted west and that it was "darkening up". . . a signal for everybody to get out and shoo the half-wild Plymouth Rock hens into a dozen weathered lean-tos.

As farm readers have already surmised, the old folks seldom saw anything larger than a five-dollar bill. But what is poverty when there are bushels of potatoes in the root cellar and flitches of bacon hanging in the smokehouse? The milk and eggs always provided enough for a new pair of "gum boots," a pledge to the church, or a quart of vanilla ice cream from the supply store. (Mixed, on Sunday afternoon after the croquet game, with homemade root beer to make "black cow" sodas.)

Evening came with a flight of hundreds of crows, beating for the roosting woods beyond the sleepy river. You began to hear farmers calling their hogs—Ben Osborn's "Whoooeeee!," burly Levi Holst's bawling "Wheeeeeaaaww!" There was a great squealing rush of pigs as Uncle Charley banged corn ears into a metal bushel and poured slop into the wooden hog trough. Then it was time for milking, with the white streams ringing in the pails, the one-eyed farm cats creeping in for the enameled pan of frothy largesse.

Supper was in the soft dark under a fake Tiffany kerosene lamp with an irresistible glass bead fringe. For a while we would sit on the lawn with Uncle Charley, smelling the hot hay wind . . . Aunt Grace had already begun to yawn before she put on her reading spectacles and sat down with the crossword puzzle or her worn Bible. Half an hour and she began to snore, not a nerve twitching in the peace of her tired soul. . . .

Nobody would set an alarm clock in a countryside full of boastful roosters. By nine o'clock a strange, delicious weariness made it easy for even a fidgeting boy to unlace his tennis shoes, put aside his copy of *Black Beauty* or *The Bobbsey Twins at the Farm* and go to sleep.

It wasn't until years later that we realized how lucky we were to have savored the good simplicity of life in the country in the last years of a pioneer pocket in the American Middle West. ❧

Country Child

Ruth DeLong Peterson

We had playgrounds all our own—
The cool green groves and rolling hills,
The shadowed pools where minnows lurked,
The meadows edged with daisy frills.

Ours were the berries and the nuts,
The trees to climb and brooks to wade,
The grapevine swings for daring swoops,
And grassy couches in the shade.

Where the sumac made a house
A child could dine if he were able
To find a stone, some grape-leaf plates
And acorn cups to set a table.

The berry stains washed off our lips,
But beauty lingers in our eyes
Through all these years when we recall
Our childhood's woodland paradise.

Goin' Fishin'

Mrs. Roy L. Peifer

On a day that's bright and sunny
    When the skies are blue and fair
And the errant little breezes
    Want to tangle up your hair,
Then I like to dig some wiggly worms;
    To take a line and pole,
And with him trudging there beside me,
    Seek a deep old fishin' hole.

For on a golden summer day
    When grasses tall are swishin'
My greatest joy's to take my boy,
    My little fellow, fishin'.

Oh, I like to wade an icy stream
    With solitude about;
With all my fancy fishing gear,
    To bag a rainbow trout.
And I like to sail the ocean
    Where white-capped breakers roar—

Go fishin' then with other men
    Miles away from shore.
But for peace and real contentment
    Now what more could I be wishin'
Than golden summer days to take
    My little fellow fishin',

Bent pin on stick, his step is quick
    And joyful here beside me;
His face is bright, his eyes alight,
    His skipping footsteps guide me.
Oh little lad, your happy dad
    Could ask no greater pleasure:
The day is fine, your hand's in mine
    And life's a golden treasure.

A day to share, forgetting care—
    Poor is the man who's missin'
This greatest joy, to take a boy,
    A little fellow, fishin'.

Getting the Cows

Ruth M. Rasey

He trudges, whistling, up the pasture lane,
As chore time nears, to fetch the cows again.
Though sweat and hayseed prickle down his back,
Old Shep is at his heels, and silvery black,
The meadow swimming hole awaits their run
And gleeful splash, as two hides cheat the sun.
A groundhog chuckles, having won the race
To den-deep safety, where the two give chase;
And empty echoes greet their hopeful search
For ring-eyed wonder in a hollow birch;
But treasure lies between the dark and them—
A skull, some foxfire, and a puffball gem,
A basswood whistle and a turtle shell.
The wood road tinkles with his heifer's bell
And life is sweet as hay in new-filled mows
When boy and dog stroll homeward with the cows.

Mama's Butter Churn

Loy C. Guy

When Bossie chewed her summer cud
She gave her very best;
Mom soundly whipped the curds and whey
With vigor, vim, and zest.

Redwood proud and hickory strong
The handle smooth and stout,
She twirled the paddle left and right
To coax the butter out.

The springhouse fairly overflowed
With mounds of guernsey gold;
Mom shared with neighbors and with kin—
A pound was never sold.

May pastures fill with thriving herds.
Turn, wheels of progress, turn—
I'd walk a rugged country mile
For butter Mama churned.

Dandelions

Bertha L. Stone

What was it I saw by the road today,
So golden bright, so cheerily gay.
Sprinkled so thickly among the grass
Along the way that I must pass?

Was it pirate's gold that someone found
Cached away in a secret mound,
Then fled, surprised by guard at night,
Scattering coins in his hurrying flight?

Or was it the coin of fairyland
Cast abroad by a robber band,
Or the dowry of a princess fair?
Say, what is this gold that is everywhere?

PHOTO RIGHT:
FARM WAGONS AND DANDELIONS
ANTRIM, NEW HAMPSHIRE
JOHNSON'S PHOTOGRAPHY

The Song of the Meadowlark

Henry B. Knox

I listen in raptured amazement
    To a medley, as note upon note
Bursts forth in exquisite cadence
    From a dear little songster's throat.

Far out on the blossoming meadows,
    Away from all sinister strife,
The meadowlark's note is proclaiming
    His secret of love and of life.

I'm certain that all of our worries
    To him would seem very absurd,
For he is so happy in trusting
    The God who cares for each bird.

I watch for him every morning
    As he darts from his perch and away,
Awakening the dawn with his carol
    To welcome another day.

His sweetly melodious broadcast
    No mere mortal genius can phrase,
Nor lift unto God our creator
    More wonderful paeans of praise.

How often by choice I would linger
    'Neath the shade of a woodland park,
And thrill to the sweetest of music—
    The song of the meadowlark!

PHOTO RIGHT:
FIELD OF COSMOS AND
BLACK-EYED SUSANS
UNION, KENTUCKY
ADAM JONES

Spending Time in the Cotton Patch

Jeannie Alexander

I've always heard that time in the army will make a man out of a boy. I say that, in like manner, time in the cotton patch will make a Southerner out of anyone.

We had a small cotton patch right next to our house. Some years when Daddy didn't have much time for farming, we rented it out to Tip Smith for shares, but I still called it ours. In later years, when the field grew corn, or soybeans, and finally was a cow pasture, I still called it the cotton patch. Patch—not field—because there is a big difference between the two. A patch is smaller, much more friendly than a field. In a patch, you could spend all day, following the pickers around, learning things and having a good time.

In our small community, before the giant picking machines took over, the pickers were your family, friends, and neighbors. Schools were out for a week or so for cotton picking. And if your parents were really intent on bringing in four hundred pounds or more, you could have a pretty good time playing without pesky interruptions.

It's much more interesting to be in the cotton patch before you are old enough to be expected to bring a big sackful in. I didn't even have a real pick-sack. Mama sewed me up a nice one out of an old gunny sack, and she put a comfortable strap on it to go around my neck and right shoulder. I guess more than a few parents figured out if their child was right-handed or not by the shoulder he wanted to sling his pick-sack from.

When dinnertime came—maybe you call it lunchtime today—Tip would take the kids to the store, and they would get cokes and bologna and cheese sandwiches, with the bologna and cheese cut as thick as they wanted. Sometimes an old car would drive up almost into the patch and somebody's mama would bring out steaming bowls of green beans or collards and pans of corn on the cob with a big gallon jug of sweet tea, sweating in a paper sack. I always wanted to stay and share, but Mama always made me walk back home and eat our own food.

I wasn't a serious picker, so Tip would pay me whenever I quit. I usually wouldn't make it past the first weigh-up at the end of the row, so he would give me my 37 cents or so and I would play in the cotton wagon for a while. Oh, the smell of fresh-picked cotton warming in the sun! My brother Tom and I would lie down in it, dig down deep into it, hide or jump up and down until somebody got aggravated and made us stop. I don't guess it caused any harm, but it got on folks' nerves when they were working and sweating in a hot cotton patch and kids were whooping it up like that. We just climbed out of the wagon when the first one yelled at us.

The days lasted forever. I would get tired of the clothes Mama made me wear: an old shirt of my brother's, worn thin from hard wear and washing and long-sleeved to keep my arms out of the hot Alabama sun and to keep me from getting all scratched up by the sharp cotton bolls; an old straw hat, because everybody knows you can cook your brain if your head gets too hot from staying in the sun all

day; long, worn jeans that once belonged to my brother, also. I don't think there was any such thing as girls' jeans—I never saw any. I wanted to wear one of my prettiest sundresses that Mama had sewed. It was too hot in those old long clothes. Soon I'd be sitting under a shade tree at the edge of the field with my sleeves and britches legs rolled up. Mama was too busy picking cotton to notice.

In the evening, there was exhilaration in the cotton patch. Now that the sun was gone, the relief from its heat was freedom. There was a sense of pride in a day's work done, and there was the wagon piled high with cotton, ready for the gin.

I learned about work, cooperation, and about life in the cotton patch. I heard enough gossip to learn how it hurts, how it heals, how it shares, how it misinforms. I learned how people were different and how they were the same. I grew up in the cotton patch, and I grew up Southern. Anybody would. ❧

Watermelon Patch

Ottis Shirk

We used to have secluded
Every summer on the farm
A spot we kept protected
From the pilferer, who might harm
Or vandalize this valued plot.
No fence with gate to latch—
'Twas just a family secret—
Our watermelon patch.

I remember as a youngster
How I watched the melons grow
As the vines spread out like carpet
Covering every hill and row.
How the mammoth green striped melons
Seemed to nestle in the vines
And each branch so closely matted—
With each other intertwined.

PHOTO ABOVE:
FAMILY GARDEN, 1895
PHILLIPS, WISCONSIN
STATE HISTORICAL SOCIETY OF WISCONSIN

When it came the time for ripening,
I wondered how Dad knew:
He'd thump each melon briskly
Then he'd thump his shoe.
He said, "It's just like music,
When they tune the tuning pipe;
If they all sound alike—musical—
The melon then is ripe."

I am still fond of melons,
But the pleasure's no more mine,
To thump those tempting beauties
And pull them from the vine.
And to me it seems I've never
Found any that could match
The sweetness of the melons
From our watermelon patch.

Carry Me Back to the Farm

Marjorie Holmes

On threshing day women got dinner all morning and washed dishes and got supper all afternoon. But it was all lively and rich with talk and purpose and somehow festive—the click and clatter of bone-handled knives and forks, and the heavy ironstone plates, brown-bordered with fleur-de-lis in the center, most of them as checked and lined as the faces of the women who handled them.

Supper was more fun, like a party. Though some of the men had gone home to do their chores, others worked until dark. And when at last they trooped wearily into the lamplit kitchen, they often found their wives who'd come bearing further food. More plates were crowded onto the already crowded table, new offerings of baked beans or potato salad or coleslaw added. Children were shooed outside with their heaping plates, there to resume their madly chasing games, while inside their elders sat visiting. Bone-tired as everybody was, a sense of rejoicing and celebration prevailed. More coffee was poured, more pies were cut.

All that food! All that plenty! A sense of the overflowing bins and barns was in the air. A sense of reaping some vital harvest, not only of the crops but of human effort. Friends and neighbors linked together in common triumph. The success of this day was the success of them all; and tomorrow it would be repeated down the road, and next week somewhere else. So the harvest didn't stop here, and the harvest moved in a perpetual ring of helping and sharing.

And later, carrying our flickering kerosene lamps up the steep back stairs, settling into the fluffy feather beds, we could smell the sweetness of the cut fields . . . hear the humming and chirping sounds of a summer night at the end of an epic day's labor. Everything seemed to be singing a lively little song of fulfillment and content. We didn't feel superior to country people anymore—we kind of envied them. ❧

PHOTO LEFT:
THRESHING
STATE HISTORICAL SOCIETY
OF WISCONSIN

PHOTO RIGHT:
FARMYARD WITH SILO
STATE HISTORICAL SOCIETY
OF WISCONSIN

Old Barns

Inga Gilson Caldwell

Old barns retain a mystic quality.
With high raftered beams, the scent still clings
Of fragrant clover mixed with timothy;
Between the wide spaced boards, a wind harp sings
While sunlight forms pipe organ patterns on
The spacious floor where dust motes dance at will.

Within the choir loft, in union,
Birds sing their choral music, versatile
In repertoire as any symphony.
Above a stable barn once, long ago,
A star of prophecy bent down; and so
Old barns retain a mystic quality.

The Old Stone Well

Joy Belle Burgess

It was a sultry August noon.
The air was sweet with rose perfume,
And not a zephyr was astir
In the daisied field or grove of fir.
As she walked with pail in hand
In hopeful mood over the dusty land
She marveled at the queenly rose,
Thirsty, too, but in beauty all aglow!
Then as she neared the old stone well
The venerable bucket she beheld
Ever waiting at the scene
To draw up springwater, cool and clean.

She gazed into its far-off depths
Where darkness hovered, silence crept,
And watched the bucket wend its way
Tilting, rocking past the walls of gray.
Deep within the ancient well
The oaken bucket slowly fell
Till with a splashing certainty
Her fondest hopes . . . reality!
For midst the perils of drought and sun
The bubbling spring had not succumbed.
Her heart was singing with gratitude
As her pail overflowed with its plenitude!

PHOTO LEFT:
HOLLYHOCKS AND WEATHERED BARN
BRISTOL, NEW HAMPSHIRE
JOHNSON'S PHOTOGRAPHY

Flour Bag Meals

Marilyn Kratz

We grew up in the flour sack!" That's what Dad often said when he told us about his childhood in the 1910s and 1920s. Life was hard on their farm near Scotland, in southeastern South Dakota. That fact was reflected in the simple, flour-based meals his mother fed her husband and six growing children.

Of course, they ate other foods over the span of the year. They planted a garden each spring to provide seasonal fresh produce. In bountiful years, there was enough to can for later use.

They butchered livestock in late fall to supply beef and pork. But storage of fresh meat, without the benefits of electrically produced refrigeration, was difficult. Some cuts of meat were fired and stored for a short time in crocks of lard. A quarter of fresh beef was often buried deep in the filled oats bin to await the slaughter of a hog in late winter. It was then mixed with pork to make smoked sausage. Grandma also canned as much meat as she could.

But the canned and smoked meat and the vegetables never lasted from one butchering season to the next. So, because there was no money to buy these items in town, Grandma went to the flour sack and made satisfying meals from its easy-to-store bounty.

The flour in those sacks was also the product of their own labor. Grandpa raised two kinds of wheat. The winter wheat was usually sold as a cash crop. The good durham spring wheat was used for flour.

Whenever Grandma's flour sack began to wilt with emptiness, Grandpa would fill three or four heavy, canvas grain sacks with wheat and haul them to a nearby Hutterite colony. There, shy little Hutterite children hid behind the long aproned skirts of their mothers and watched Grandpa and my dad unload the wheat.

The wheat was ground in a water powered mill. The chaff—the part we call bran and value in our health-conscious diets—was separated from the flour and fed to the pigs. So much for fiber!

The sifted flour was yellowish-gray in color. Both of my parents recalled that it seemed more flavorful than the flour we buy today.

The Hutterites provided white cotton bags in which the flour was taken home. Grandpa paid for the grinding with a bag of wheat.

Besides being nutritious and filling, the flour-based meals Grandma made were quick to prepare and did not require much attention as they cooked.

Mom recalls that each flour dish was traditionally served with its own particular accompaniment. For example, dumplings were served with meat and gravy (usually chicken), strudels were served with watermelon, prunes, or canned apples; kraut strudels had bacon added; and filled cheese buttons were covered with fried (rendered) sweet cream.

The simple dough used to create these dishes was made with eggs and milk products produced on the farm, making them even more economical. Even the yeast used in some of the dishes was "everlasting" yeast, which was kept growing in a quart jar in the cellar and replenished each time it was used.

In these days, when we are weight and health conscious, these sifted flour-based meals are not what we would choose as a large part of our diet. But, once in a while, I get hungry for them and ask Mom to make one for me. I'll share her slightly modernized versions of a few of these recipes. I think you'll agree that they have a certain "back to basics" appeal, and, even in this day, are still economical.

Dumplings

Thaw 1 loaf of frozen white bread dough (or use an equivalent amount from any bread recipe). Shape pieces of dough into long dumplings a little larger than a fat finger. Let rise (covered) until double (about a half-hour, if dough is not too cold).

Put 3 tablespoons oil or shortening into a heavy skillet. Add 2 tablespoons chopped onion. Saute until tender. Add 3 medium peeled potatoes cut into 1-inch cubes. Add salt and pepper to taste. Add water almost to top of potatoes. Bring to a boil.

Lay raised dumplings on potatoes. Cover very tightly. (Mom used to wrap a wet dishtowel around the lid of the skillet.)

Cook 15 minutes at moderate heat. Reduce heat to low and cook 15 minutes longer. Take off burner and let sit 5 minutes. Do not uncover while cooking. Serve immediately.

Strudels

Follow dumpling recipe, except shape as follows: Roll dough into about 3 large, thin rectangles. Spread with melted shortening. Roll up until about as thick as a finger. Cut off and start new roll. Cut rolls into 3-inch lengths.

Buttons (Knopf)

Mix 2 cups flour, 2 eggs, $\frac{1}{2}$-teaspoon salt, and about one-half cup milk. Add more flour, if needed to make stiff dough. Knead smooth. Snip with scissors into 1-inch bits. Drop into large kettle containing about 2 quarts of boiling salted water. (Dip scissors into boiling water often to keep the dough from sticking.) Cook 15 to 20 minutes, until tender. Drain. Serve with kraut and wieners.

Cheese Knopf

Use buttons dough. Roll about $\frac{1}{4}$-inch thick. Cut into 5-inch squares. Mix 12 ounces dry curd cottage cheese, $\frac{1}{2}$-teaspoon salt and pepper, $\frac{1}{4}$-cup chopped green onion, and 2 egg yolks. Put about $\frac{1}{4}$-cup of cheese mixture on each square. Fold corner of dough over to make closed triangle shape. Seal edges by moistening and pinching tightly.

Boil in salted water very gently about 20 minutes. Drain.

Old butter churns bring back special memories for many people. In my past, one of the most memorable moments was the time when Mama finished churning, placed the fresh butter on a plate, and covered it with the lid that had a decorative press in the top. She took it to the deep well where she pulled up the bucket. She placed the butter dish on top of the milk crock and let the bucket down just short of the water line. Milk and butter stayed ice cold.

Mae Rawles

When I was a girl, my sister and I sliced peaches and layed them neatly on a large sheet Mama had spread out on top of the roof of the smokehouse. We laid the peaches out in long straight rows. There they would dry in the hot Arkansas sun. Each night, we rolled up the sheet with the fruit and took all into the house; in the morning, we took the sheet back up to the shed roof and unrolled it. After the peaches were dried, we stored them in the root cellar where they stayed cool. Mama used them to make the best fried pies I've ever had. We had peaches all winter. Now, I make Fresh Peach Pie and the smell of the peaches as I peel and slice them is enough to send me back about seventy-five years ago to peach season in Arkansas.

Here's my recipe for fresh peach pie. In a large bowl, stir together ½ to ¾ cup sugar and 3 tablespoons flour. Add 6 cups peeled, thinly sliced ripe peaches; toss until peaches are coated with flour and sugar. Pour into a 9-inch pastry-lined pie plate. Trim bottom pastry to edge of pie plate. Roll out pastry into a 10-inch circle. Cut slits or leaf designs in top crust. Place on filling; seal and crimp edge. Brush top crust with milk and sprinkle with cinnamon-sugar. Cover edges of crust with foil. Bake in a preheated 375° oven 25 minutes. Remove foil. Bake an additional 20 minutes or until the top is golden and peaches are bubbly. Cool on a wire rack.

Mae Rawles

Queen Anne's lace is originally from Europe, has a carrot-shaped root, and is sometimes called the Wild Carrot. It may cover an entire field with clusters of small, white flowers. The central flower is often a deep purple or red.

Blackberries picked from your own garden just seem sweeter than those from the supermarket. And no dessert can beat the taste of warm blackberry cobbler topped with a scoop of vanilla ice cream. Here's an old country recipe: Preheat oven to 435°. In a large bowl, sift together ¾ cup flour, 2 teaspoons sugar, ¼ teaspoon salt, and 1½ teaspoons baking powder. Cut in 2 to 3 tablespoons chilled butter. Make a well in the center and add, all at once, ½ cup half-and-half. Stir to mix until dough forms a soft ball. Set aside. In a saucepan, combine 3 cups blackberries, ⅔ cup sugar, and 1 tablespoon flour. Bring mixture to a boil. Pour into an 8-inch baking dish; spoon dough over top. Bake 30 minutes. Serve warm with a scoop of vanilla ice cream.

Red in the morning
Sailors take warning.
Red at night,
Sailors delight.

When the dew is on the grass,
Rain will seldom come to pass.
When the grass is dry at morning light,
Look for rain before the night.

If the moon shows a
silver shield,
Be not afraid to reap
your field;
But if she rises haloed
round,
Soon we'll tread on
deluged ground.

Country Memories

Joyce M. Rattray

Every sticky summer day in the city brings back a certain longing for those summers spent at my aunt's country home long ago. It lay nestled beneath an escarpment in a valley amid the Niagara fruit belt. Just thinking about those summers startles a thousand recollections and brings the sweet fragrance of the fruit trees back to me. No matter how hot the day was, the old farmhouse tucked into the mountains always remained cool.

We played among the trees, climbing them if we so felt, and eating the sweet fruit at will. There were acres of playground in which to run, and limitless places to hide in the orchards. There was a deep sense of peace and joy at life itself locked within that fertile valley. The fields were aglow with the vibrant colors of wildflowers which grew everywhere in mass profusion. The fragrance of the fruit trees filled the valley with an intoxicating perfume not to be found anywhere else I have been since. And behind it all the dark mountains loomed against the landscape, somber and majestic they rose, sprinkled throughout with tall, dark trees, engulfed in shadow.

My aunt was a pastry chef for one of the golf and country clubs back in the 1920s. Many a gala wedding took place for which she did all the baking. There was nothing like coming indoors to those tantalizing aromas. It didn't matter what she was baking, she always took the time to let the children get their fingers in and help.

Her specialty was wedding cakes. It was every bride's dream for miles around to have one of my aunt's five-story-high wedding cakes adorning their head table. These cakes were made one month ahead of time and stored in her big freezer.

It was with a great love of doing something for someone else that all the mixing and beating took place. The children were allowed to get the tin canisters down from her pantry. These containers were all brightly decorated by her own hands with pictures of whatever they contained in them. There were cans of raisins, and candied citron, currents, and almonds, all kept fresh by the tightly sealed containers. Then there were the neat rows of jars lining her shelves. Each held its own pungent smelling spice, neatly labeled and topped with a handmade quilted cover. It took two of us to haul out the fifteen-pound flour container; when the lid was removed a soft cloud of white powder floated lazily to the ground to settle into the cracks in the pine floor.

With great ceremony each child added the ingredient that had been carefully measured out for us. Then that enormous wooden spoon would once more continue the beating and mixing. We stood back in awe as my aunt lifted the large sieve down from the cupboard and sifted twelve cups of flour into the ever-growing mixture. Then five different-sized cake pans were lined up—largest to smallest, all lined with heavy brown paper. At last the final ingredient was added. The ingredient, she said with a chuckle, that a wedding cake wouldn't be complete without—one ounce of whiskey. With big eyes we watched the wooden spoon

sweep the bowl one last time. By this time the bowl was so heavy several of us had to help as she poured the rich mixture into the waiting pans.

As the last of her pans went into her oversized oven we were all banned from the kitchen while the cleanup took place. The next three hours were spent either playing in the orchards or sneaking up the stairs to the attic. The air in the attic stairwell was suffocating and once we reached the attic above it was only slightly better. Inside the attic was a whole lifetime of memories. We spent many hours in that shadowy room telling our favorite ghost stories.

But at last the time came for which we all waited—the icing of the cake. A mountain of icing was set on the table and we gathered around as she performed her work of art. Elaborate swirls and pink flowers appeared as if by magic. Layer was placed upon layer— each receiving the same careful attention. When at last the final layer was complete, my aunt went to her special drawer where the tiny brides and grooms lay in their plastic wrapper. She chose the happy couple to top the cake and stood back to survey the finishing touch.

There it stood. In all its splendor. A five-story magnificent work of art—all forty-five pounds of it!

All that baking and licking bowls clean with our fingers soon took its toll on our young bodies; after climbing into that big bed and snuggling down beneath the quilts it was morning in an instant.

The patient way that my aunt let each and every one of us help her comes back to me today as my own three children stand around me in my kitchen, and I remember that there is always room for one more finger in the bowl!

Always Remembering

Maysie Tuley Newsom

I believe that every child who has not spent some time on a farm, either visiting or living there, has missed a great deal in life. No vacation that I ever had has thrilled me quite as much as my trips to the country each summer when I was a little girl.

Back of our country house was an apple orchard, and blueberries grew at the far edge of the woods, beyond the barn. At the barn I talked to the horses or climbed into the haymow to sink down on the fragrant hay for awhile. It was fun to run through the great piles of grain in the granary, popping some of it in my mouth to chew; and it was exciting to gather eggs and to watch the milking. In June, we picked daisies and wild strawberries. Down the road a bit and under a bridge was a quiet, clear, cool, creek where I could wade or just sit and watch the minnows scurry by.

Perhaps my fondest memory of farm life, however, is the food. How good it was in the country! At noon, after ringing the bell atop the tall pole in the yard, I ate a bountiful dinner. At night after the chores were done, a supper of hashed brown potatoes, succulent fried pork, and platters of fried eggs waited—all we wanted to eat. Food has never since tasted so good to me. We finished with apple pie or whatever fruit was ripe at the time—strawberries, blackberries, huckleberries, or peaches—all served in a big bowl with plenty of cream. And, of course, always a big pitcher of milk kept cool in the cellar and from which we drank all we could hold.

Later, in the quiet of the evening, we all sat on the porch and talked of the day's work, the crops, and the weather. But a little girl, filled with wonders of her new world, listened mostly to the katydids and dreamed of tomorrow. 🦋

PHOTO ABOVE:
HEREFORDS AMONG BLUEBONNETS
TEXAS HILL COUNTRY
MARBLE FALLS, TEXAS
ADAM JONES

The Barefoot Boy

James Whitcomb Riley

Blessings on thee, little man,
Barefoot boy, with cheek of tan!
With thy turned up pantaloons,
And thy merry whistled tunes;
With thy red lips, redder still
Kissed by strawberries on the hill;
With the sunshine in thy face,
Through thy torn brim's jaunty grace;
From my heart I give thee joy,—
I was once a barefoot boy!

Prince thou art,—the grown-up man
Only is republican.
Let the million-dollared ride!
Barefoot, trudging at his side,
Thou hast more than he can buy
In the reach of ear and eye,—
Outward sunshine, inward joy:
Blessings on thee, barefoot boy!

Oh for boyhood's painless play,
Sleep that wakes in laughing day,
Health that mocks the doctor's rules,
Knowledge never learned in schools,
Of the wild bee's morning chase.
Of the wildflower's time and place,
Flight of fowl and habitude
Of the tenants of the wood;
How the tortoise bears his shell,
How the woodchuck digs his cell,
And the ground mole sinks his well;
How the robin feeds her young,
How the oriole's nest is hung;
Where the whitest lilies blow,
Where the freshest berries grow,
Where the ground nut trails its vine,

Where the wood-grape's clusters shine;
Of the black wasp's cunning way,
Mason of his walls of clay,
And the architectural plans
Of gray hornet artisans!
For, eschewing books and tasks,
Nature answers all he asks;
Hand in hand with her he walks,
Face to face with her he talks,
Part and parcel of her joy,—
Blessings on the barefoot boy!

Oh for boyhood's time of June,
Crowding years in one brief moon,
When all things I heard or saw,
Me, their master, waited for.
I was rich in flowers and trees,
Humming-birds and honey-bees;
For my sport the squirrel played,
Plied the snouted mole his spade;
For my taste the blackberry cone
Purpled over hedge and stone;
Laughed the brook for my delight
Through the day and through the night,
Whispering at the garden wall,
Talked with me from fall to fall;
Mine the sand-rimmed pickerel pond,
Mine the walnut slopes beyond,
Mine, on bending orchard trees,
Apples of Hesperides!
Still as my horizon grew,
Larger grew my riches, too;
All the world I saw or knew
Seemed a complex Chinese toy,
Fashioned for a barefoot boy! . . .

PHOTO LEFT:
BOY AT PUMP

In the Shade of the Old Apple Tree

HARRY H. WILLIAMS

EGBERT VAN ALSTYNE

Arranged by Dick Torrans

1. The o - ri - ole with joy was sweet-ly sing-ing, The lit-tle brook was bab - 'ling it's tune, The
2. I've real-ly come a long way from the cit - y, And tho my heart is breaking I'll be brave, I've

vil - lage bells at noon were gai-ly ringing The world seemed bright-er than a har-vest moon; For
brought this bunch of flowers, I think they're pret-ty, To place up - on a fresh-ly mould-ed grave. If

there with-in my arms I gent-ly pressed you And blush-ing red, you slow-ly turned a - way, I
you will show me, fa-ther, where she's ly - ing, Or if it's far just point it out to me, Said

can't for - get the way I once ca - ressed you, I on - ly pray we'll meet an-oth-er day. In the
he, "she told us all when she was dy-ing, To bur-y her be - neath the ap - ple tree."

shade of the old ap-ple tree,_____ Where the love in your eyes I could see,_____ When the

voice that I heard, like the song of the bird, Seemed to whis-per sweet mu-sic to me;_____ I could

hear the dull buzz of the bee,_____ In the blossoms as you said to me,_____ With a

heart that is true, I'll be wait-ing for you, In the shade of the old ap-ple tree._____

Sunset on the Farm

Cleo King

When the afternoon is waning
   and the sun is slipping low,
Then I often stop my farm chores
   just to watch the sunset glow;
How I glory in the beauty
   of those ever-changing rays,
Splashing rose and gold and purple
   in a panoramic blaze
That envelops earth and heaven
   with a miracle of light
As it flashes bold defiance
   to the fast-approaching night!

Oh, it seems to me there's nothing
   that can have an equal charm
Or has quite the same attraction
   as a sunset on the farm;
Something in its magic splendor,
   coming at the close of day,
Has a way of making troubles
   seem unreal and far away;
Tensions ease and almost vanish
   when those last, long shadows fall,
And the heart bows in reverence to
   the wonder of it all.

PHOTO RIGHT:
*SHENANDOAH RIVER VALLEY FARMLAND
IN EARLY FALL*
FRONT ROYAL, VIRGINIA
JOHNSON'S PHOTOGRAPHY